RFK
1925 – 1968

RFK
1925 – 1968
JAMES A. HUDSON

SBS SCHOLASTIC BOOK SERVICES
New York Toronto London Auckland Sydney

CONTENTS

"Some men see things as they are and say, 'Why?'
I dream of things that never were and say, 'Why not?' "

ROBERT F. KENNEDY
(after Bernard Shaw)

1 THE LAST CAMPAIGN

June 5, 1968. Jubilant, he threaded his way through the crowd toward the podium. All the shouting, the applause, the popping flashbulbs were for him. He was the winner.

Beside him was his wife. Bodyguards made a pathway through the crowd for the couple. But occasionally the candidate stopped and reached into the crowd to shake a hand, flashing the familiar boyish smile.

A few weeks earlier, in the Oregon Presidential primary, he had tasted defeat — a new experience for him. It had, in fact, been the first defeat suffered by him or his two brothers in 27 primary and general election campaigns. But now, after a hard fight in California, he had won this state's Democratic primary election. Once more he was the victor.

As he made his way through the cheering people in Los Angeles' Ambassador Hotel, he may have

None of the strain of campaigning shows as Bobby Kennedy celebrates his victory in the California Presidential primary, June 5, 1968. Just behind him is his wife Ethel.

thought of his brother, the late President. Certainly many of those watching did. There was the same youthful charm, the same energy, even the same vocal mannerisms. In 1960, John F. Kennedy had led his party to victory. Now eight years later, with a younger Kennedy at the helm, it was all happening again.

For Robert F. Kennedy there was reason enough to celebrate in the early morning hours of June 5, 1968. During his ill-fated Oregon campaign, he had ignored his opponent, Senator Eugene McCarthy. He had concentrated his criticism, instead, on the candidate considered most likely to receive the nomination, Vice President Hubert Humphrey. But after his Oregon defeat, Kennedy had changed tactics.

Previously he had sidestepped McCarthy's challenge to debate him. Now he accepted it. During the televised argument, the two candidates argued the Viet Nam issue — specifically, the possible role of the National Liberation Front (the political arm of the Viet Cong) in the postwar Saigon government. It may have been that Kennedy showed up to more advantage in this debate than did McCarthy. Or perhaps Kennedy might have won the primary in any event, thanks to his popularity with minority groups. In any case he must have been doing something right. Because now the hard campaigning, the tiring days and sleepless nights were paying off. With 20,731 of California's 21,302 precincts counted, he led McCarthy by 1,402,911 votes to 1,267,608.

Many political observers said that his was a futile fight. They said the Presidential candidate would be chosen, as always, by the regular party faithful, the convention delegates. They said that no matter who

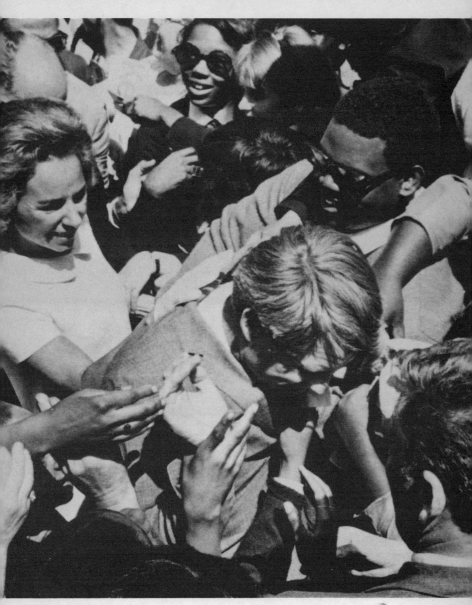

In Detroit, Kennedy and his wife try to make their way through a noon-time crowd at a rally where he was to speak.

Above: Kennedy and his opponent, Senator Eugene McCarthy (second from left), debate issues on television in California. *Below:* The candidate visits a child-care center in Oregon.

Ethel Kennedy shakes hands with Martin Luther King III, son of the assassinated civil rights leader. The Kennedys had just arrived in Atlanta, Georgia, for Dr. King's funeral.

The Kennedys are welcomed in a Wyoming April snowstorm.

won the primaries, no matter how much public support he gained, he couldn't win the nomination. People said Hubert Humphrey would get the nomination because he was favored by President Johnson and the party "bosses."

Robert Kennedy refused to believe this. Show the political bosses how strongly the people support you, he reasoned, and they won't dare ignore the public's choice. Show them that the "little man" is for you, that the worker supports you, that the minorities have given you their mandate. . . . Show them that the poor have confidence in you, and the bosses will give way.

When Kennedy reached the podium, Ethel was at his side. Perhaps even more than most candidates' wives, she had earned her place beside the winner. For wherever Bobby had been, usually Ethel had been there too — whether it had been to greet the enthusiastic crowds, or to share the sorrow of the family of a civil rights leader assassinated less than two months earlier.

One of the curiosities of politics is the charm that the Kennedys held for the poor. Other men born to wealth and privilege have held sway over the multitudes. Franklin Delano Roosevelt was elected to the White House more often than any other man, thanks in large extent to the appeal he had for the masses.

But Roosevelt, with his famous cigarette holder, his pince-nez glasses, his cultivated voice and precise diction, never let his audience forget his aristocratic background. Despite his many social reforms, FDR seemed remote from the working man. He was more like an ideal to be aspired to, rather than a living, breathing human being to be touched.

The Kennedys were different. Crowds sometimes

nearly tore them apart with affection. It was true that the Kennedy brothers were rich. But somehow the poor claimed them as their own.

People called this phenomenon "the Kennedy charm."

Few disagreed that Bobby — sometimes called "cold" and "ruthless" by his opponents — seemed to have even more of this remarkable quality than his elder brother, Jack.

It was difficult, seeing Bobby Kennedy in person, to believe that a shrewd politician, a strong-willed fighter lived behind that shy, boyish manner. He looked like a young man just home from college.

The young, as well as the poor, responded to him. If "Don't trust anyone over 30" was their slogan, they nevertheless seemed willing enough to trust Bobby who, at 43, had long ago passed beyond this age barrier. His youthful good looks, his zest for living, his refusal to accept the status quo made him one of them.

Few of his admirers ever claimed that Bobby Kennedy was the sort to risk all for a noble cause. He was, rather, a tough and able political strategist. By nature impetuous, he had learned when to speak out and when to bide his time. While it is undeniable that his tactics were designed to make Robert Kennedy win it could be argued that they were also designed to make sure the principles he believed in would succeed. Exactly how big a role those principles played in determining his actions was a point endlessly disputed. But while partisans and skeptics argued, the crowds turned out by the thousands and hundreds of thousands to cheer Bobby Kennedy.

On June 4, in California, they turned out to vote for him.

Youthful admirers pursue Kennedy at New York's JFK Airport.

Now, in the early hours of June 5, he was standing at the podium in the hotel ballroom, making his victory speech, thanking his campaign workers for helping to make it all possible, spurring them on to more victories in the coming months. "On to Chicago and let's win there," he said.

When he had finished speaking he started to leave the ballroom. But he and his aides found the crush of well-wishers to be overwhelming. They couldn't make their way through. Instead of proceeding back through the ballroom crowd, as planned, they hastily adopted another escape route. It was an ill-fated decision.

For after Kennedy and his party had hurried through the hotel kitchen and were striding down a hallway they hadn't expected they'd use, gunshots rang out.

A moment later, Kennedy lay sprawled upon the floor, critically wounded.

A day later, he died.

To Americans, Kennedy's death was like living with a nightmare from which there was no awakening. Twice within two months a loved and respected leader had been felled by senseless hatred. On April 4, in Memphis, Tennessee, Martin Luther King, Jr., was killed. And with the loss of a young and vigorous President still a painful scar on their memories, people watched unbelieving as his younger brother was brought down — like him — in the midst of celebration, and carried to a nearby grave.

In millions of living rooms, the same veiled, frozen faces moved across the TV screen. Within the public tragedy of a powerful nation reduced again to helpless mourning by the action of a diseased mind, there lay the private tragedy of a powerful and gifted family who seemed marked by the fates for destruction.

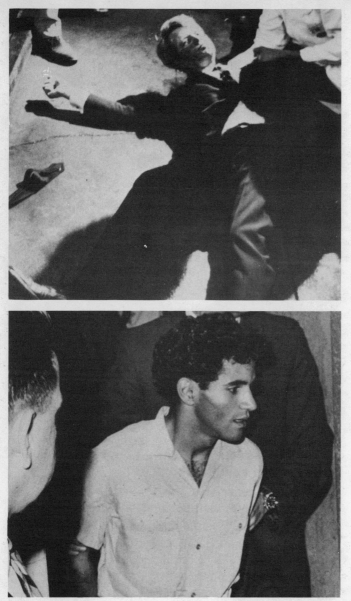

The wounded Kennedy and his accused assassin, Sirhan Sirhan.

2 GROWING UP A KENNEDY

Robert Francis Kennedy was born on November 20, 1925. He was the seventh of Rose and Joseph P. Kennedy's nine children. "When you come from that far down," he once remarked, "you have to struggle to survive."

Merely to survive wasn't exactly what Joseph Kennedy had in mind for his sons. Struggling was all right, if it was necessary to reach the goal. But victory — not survival — was what the Kennedy boys would achieve, if their father had his way. And he did.

"Win, win, win." For Joe Kennedy, the father, this was more than a desirable goal — it was practically a moral obligation. To compromise, he felt, was to lose. "If you've got a second choice," he was fond of saying, "then you haven't got a first choice." From early childhood, the Kennedy children were impressed with the necessity of going "all out" in everything they

The Kennedys in 1937. To Joseph Kennedy's left are Patricia and John. Seated are Jean (front) and Eunice. With Mrs. Kennedy are Joe, Jr., and Rosemary (right), Bobby (by fireplace), Kathleen, and Edward.

did. Their driving competitiveness first found expression in sports, particularly in boisterous games of touch football. Later this competitiveness was to make the Kennedys the political phenomenon of their time.

Joe Kennedy's pride and aggressiveness stemmed from the fact that his family had pulled themselves up by their own bootstraps. The first member to arrive in this country was Patrick Kennedy, who fled Ireland's Great Famine and settled in Boston in 1848. Within four generations, the Kennedys would transform themselves from poor, despised Irish immigrants into the First Family of the land.

Patrick's son, Patrick Jr., was the first native-born Kennedy. He managed a saloon and made enough money from it to send his son Joseph to Harvard. By the time he was 25, Joseph Kennedy had become a bank president and had amassed nearly a million dollars. In 1914, young Kennedy — who was to become Bobby's father — married the belle of Boston Irish society. She was Rose Fitzgerald, daughter of Joseph F. ("Honey Fitz") Fitzgerald — another ambitious man who had fought his way up from Boston's Irish wards to become the city's mayor.

Joseph Kennedy, also, was active in public life. He served on the Securities and Exchange Commission and, in return for his support of Franklin D. Roosevelt, he was named Ambassador to England — at London's Court of St. James.

The head of the Kennedy family had already decided that, no matter how big a mark he made in life, his sons would make bigger ones. To free them from financial worries, he set up million-dollar trust funds for each of his children. He thus made it possible for them

While his father was U.S. Ambassador to Britain, Bobby had a chance to develop his interests. Here, he and his sister Kathleen are out for a morning ride in a London park.

to be idle the rest of their lives — if they so chose. But the Kennedy upbringing, the need to excel, made such a choice unlikely.

The father's greatest hopes were pinned on his eldest son, Joe Jr. An excellent scholar, a fine athlete, a handsome, outgoing, ambitious youth, Joe was almost a legend in his own family. It was assumed that he would accomplish great things. With a little "coaching" from his father, Joe confided to close friends his intention to become President of the United States.

The Kennedy ideal of service to the country was not limited to running for its highest office. During World War II, all the Kennedy boys who were old enough — Joe, Jack, and Bobby — enlisted in the Navy. Joe was commissioned a pilot and flew many bombing missions over Europe. During one mission, while over the English Channel, his plane exploded. The war had put an end to the promise of Joe Kennedy, Jr.

While the Kennedys mourned the loss of their brightest hope, the grieving father began preparing Jack to take his place. The boys took this succession of responsibility for granted. "Just as I went into politics when Joe died," said Senator John Kennedy, several years later, "if anything happened to me tomorrow my brother Bobby would run for my seat." Jack had, at first, no special love of politics. But he had already shown himself a leader. A year before Joe's death, John had been reported missing in action in the Pacific. The skipper of a PT boat, he and his 12-man crew were cast adrift after a Japanese destroyer rammed and sank their small craft. Two crew members died. But Kennedy saved three men from drowning and led his remaining crew to safety and rescue a week later.

"Goodwill ambassadors" Bobby (left) and Teddy receive souvenirs from zoo official Julian Huxley after opening the children's section of the London Zoo.

Above: Robert Kennedy is sworn into the Navy by Lt. Cmdr. Edward Brewer. *Opposite page:* He looks on (far right) as his

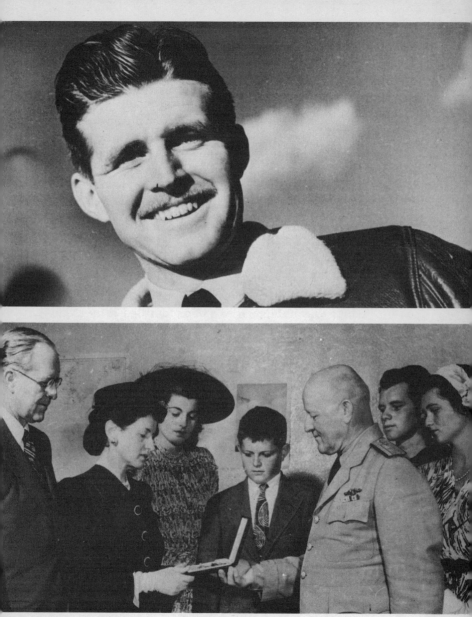

parents accept the Navy Cross, awarded posthumously to his
brother Joe (above), who was killed while flying a mission.

At the time, Bobby was attending naval officer candidate school. The example of Jack's heroism and, later, the loss of Joe strengthened his determination to play an active part in the war. He managed to get himself released from officer candidate school, was made a seaman second class, and was assigned to a new destroyer, the *Joseph P. Kennedy Jr.* The ship, however, spent the duration of the war cruising around in the Caribbean, and Bobby returned home with no heroic exploits behind him.

Upon his discharge from the Navy, Bobby Kennedy attended Harvard — by now a family tradition. Both Joe Jr. and Jack had gone to Harvard. Joe had excelled in sports and studies and been elected to a number of offices. Jack, after a slow start, had been graduated with honors and had written an outstanding paper which was published as a book, entitled *Why England Slept.* Both brothers were — as they say in show business — "hard acts to follow."

In his prep school days, Bobby had shown himself to be only an average scholar, and this picture did not change at Harvard. "I didn't go to class very much . . ." he once said, "I used to talk and argue a lot, mostly about sports and politics."

He devoted most of his energies to sports. Football was a passion with him. Though he weighed only 150 pounds and was but five-feet-ten inches tall, he drove himself and became captain of the freshman team. Eventually he made the varsity, and in a game with Harvard's archenemy, Yale, he was sent in to play in the last moments. Harvard was beaten mercilessly — but Bobby Kennedy had won his letter.

While still at Harvard, Bobby got his first strong taste of politics. He campaigned for his brother Jack,

At Harvard, Bobby Kennedy played back on the football team. Here, he relaxes outside the Varsity Club with (l. to r.) John Fiorentino, end, Jim Noonan and Frank Miklos, backs.

The newly married Bobby and his bride, the former Ethel Skakel, at their wedding reception at the Skakel home.

who ran for Congress in 1946 — and was elected. "Bobby always took the toughest jobs," observed another campaigner, Dave Powers. "No one ever worked so hard . . . to have his brother elected as Bobby Kennedy did."

After being graduated from Harvard in 1948, with a major in government, Bobby showed signs of a restlessness which was characteristic of him. He went to the Middle East for a while and covered the Arab-Israeli war as a correspondent for the *Boston Post*. Then he decided to attend the University of Virginia Law School. At Virginia he became president of the student forum and brought many distinguished speakers to the campus.

Still no class "brain," he was graduated 56th in a class of 124 at law school. But a school friend remembered something about him that his class standing alone doesn't indicate. "Bob had an intensity and seriousness of purpose that struck you immediately," he said. "There was very little wasted motion in Bobby Kennedy. . . ."

In 1944, Bobby had gone on a ski trip to Canada where he met another energetic personality. Her name was Ethel Skakel. She and Bobby had many things in common. Their backgrounds were similiar: both came from large New England Catholic families. Her father, like his, was a self-made millionaire. She, too, was a sports enthusiast and drove herself relentlessly. At the time, however, she was more outgoing than Bobby, who was often considered shy.

The couple was married in St. Mary's Roman Catholic Church in Ethel's hometown, Greenwich, Connecticut, on June 17, 1950.

3 WITH SLEEVES ROLLED UP

When Bobby and his bride returned from a honeymoon in Hawaii, he still had a year of study before being graduated from the University of Virginia Law School. He rented a three-bedroom house near the campus and studied incessantly throughout the week so that he and Ethel would be free for the weekend.

On many weekends, they would have houseguests — friends or members of their families who came down to visit them. The gregarious Ethel had a large number of friends and, like her husband, plenty of relatives.

"They entertained a good deal," recalled one friend. "On typical evenings, we'd have the men at one end of the room discussing law and the women at the other discussing babies." Years later, at their estate near Washington, the Robert Kennedys would become noted for their parties at which guests could

Senator Joseph McCarthy (center), with Democratic Senator Stuart Symington, a member of his investigating subcommittee, and Robert Kennedy, committee minority counsel.

expect the unexpected: a sudden duck in the pool, perhaps, or a game of touch football in evening clothes.

Bobby had not been out of law school two years when he got involved in controversy. He had started his career quietly enough, working for a modest salary in the Justice Department. In 1952, he had returned to Massachusetts to manage his brother Jack's successful campaign for the Senate.

Then, in 1953, Bobby Kennedy made what many critics still regard as a mistake. He accepted a position as a staff member of the Senate Investigation Subcommittee, headed by the late Senator Joseph McCarthy, an old friend of the Kennedy family.

At the time Robert Kennedy joined the subcommittee staff, Joseph McCarthy was at the height of his power. The subcommittee's chief target was alleged Communists in government.

A few months after joining the investigating group, Kennedy was making headlines. He investigated reports that Allied countries who were at war in Korea against the Communist Chinese were also shipping goods to Communist China — and he found these reports to be true.

His friends are convinced that Kennedy thought he could do his country a service by joining forces with the subcommittee. In fact, he later said, "I felt it was work that needed to be done then." It soon became apparent to him, however, that the work was being done the wrong way. For the Senator's use of innuendo and unproved charges was ruining the reputations of many persons and creating a climate of fear within the country.

Fed up with the tactics of McCarthy and his aides,

Above: with Senator Karl Mundt (Rep.) a member of the sub-committee. *Below:* with committee chairman Joseph McCarthy.

Bobby resigned from his committee job after six months. But his political enemies were already beginning to call him "ruthless" — a charge which he was to hear again and again during his career.

Although sensitive to such criticism, Bobby often tried to joke about it. Before leaving for work one day, he took the morning newspaper upstairs to his wife. Coming back downstairs, he smilingly told a friend, "Well, that's my good deed for the day. Now I can go back to being my ruthless self."

Those who knew Bobby intimately saw another side of him. "Bobby is soft, soft on people," his father once said. "He has the capacity to be emotionally involved, to feel things deeply. . . ." While he made no attempt to hide his animosity toward some people, he showed himself to be a steadfast friend to those people he did like.

When, during the 1960 Presidential campaign, the civil rights leader Dr. Martin Luther King, Jr., was jailed on parole violation charges, it was Bobby who telephoned the Georgia judge and secured King's release. It wasn't necessarily considered "smart politics" at the time for the Kennedys to get so involved with King. Jack's position among white Southern Democrats was by no means secure. But Bobby knew what had to be done. (Later, this impulsive act was credited with winning Jack many Negro votes.)

For a half a year, Bobby Kennedy worked for the Hoover Commission, making a study designed to increase the effectiveness of the executive branch of the government. But then he returned to the McCarthy committee — this time as counsel to the committee's Democratic minority members. As such, he began attacking the methods employed by

Bobby and Ethel on their return from an extensive tour of the Soviet Union in September 1955. At the time he was chief counsel of the Senate Government Operations Committee.

McCarthy's aides, Roy Cohn and David Schine. McCarthy was finally censured by the Senate, and his career as a Communist-hunter was left in tatters.

Kennedy remained friends with McCarthy, though he disagreed with his methods. He blamed Cohn and Schine for most of the committee's abuses. And when McCarthy died a broken man, in 1957, Robert Kennedy flew to Wisconsin to attend this controversial man's funeral.

In 1954, after the Democrats had taken control of Congress, Kennedy became the committee's chief counsel, under Arkansas' Senator McClellan. For a couple of years, business was fairly routine. Then Bobby became embroiled in another fight. Soon he was making new enemies.

Spurred by newspaper reports that there was corruption in the leadership of the International Brotherhood of Teamsters, Chauffeurs, Warehouse Men, and Helpers of America, the committee began investigating. A special new committee (soon dubbed the "Rackets Committee") was formed to study improper activity in this and other unions, as well as in some businesses. Among the committee members was Senator John F. Kennedy.

For more than two years, Bobby and the other investigators probed the charges of misconduct among labor leaders. Their investigation of the Teamsters' Union turned up enough evidence of larceny and other crimes within the union leadership to result in the ouster and jailing of the union's president, David Beck.

Then Bobby took on an even more formidable antagonist, Beck's successor as union president, James R. Hoffa.

Kennedy was a dedicated foe of James R. Hoffa, right, the president of the Teamsters Union. Some people called Bobby "ruthless" because of his determination to "get Hoffa."

Bobby, counsel for the Senate committtte investigating racket-eering in the Teamsters Union, confers with his brother, Senator John F. Kennedy, a committee member, at a hearing.

Hoffa, a self-made man who sneered at Kennedy as "this kid," was an elusive target. Many times when Kennedy asked him pointed questions during committee hearings, Hoffa's memory seemed to go blank. During one memorable session, Hoffa had more than one hundred such memory failures.

Some people began to criticize Bobby Kennedy for his increasingly sharp attacks on Hoffa during these sessions. Hoffa sometimes seemed to relish making Kennedy "look bad."

The labor leader once quipped: "If this kid doesn't get away from this crusade, he's going to crack up."

It would take seven years to convict Hoffa. In March 1964, the union leader was convicted of attempted bribery and, three years later, after numerous appeals were turned down, he was imprisoned.

In 1959, however, Hoffa was still at liberty, and Bobby Kennedy had new business on his mind. He left the Rackets Committee and began to plan a strategy for a larger goal.

When John F. Kennedy decided to run for the office of President in the 1960 election, he didn't have to look far for a campaign manager. He chose his younger brother because, said JFK, Bobby was "the best man for the job." In this capacity, Bobby probably did more to put his brother into the White House than did any other man — including Jack himself.

At least that's what most political experts said. And "Old Joe Kennedy," seemed to agree. "Jack works as hard as any man can," he once said. "Bobby goes a little farther."

Bobby faced an extremely difficult task. A number

of factors weighed heavily against the Kennedys.

First, they had to overcome the prejudice — still found to some extent in certain parts of the nation — against Catholics. Never before had a Catholic been elected President. Historians agreed generally that the religious issue had played a big part in the 1928 election. In that contest, Alfred E. Smith, a Catholic, had been defeated in his bid for the White House by Herbert Hoover.

Jack's age also was regarded as a strike against him. At 42, he would be the youngest man ever elected to the nation's highest office. His critics used his age as an argument that he was too inexperienced for the job.

Then, too, there was JFK's personality. Dignified to the point of aloofness, he was far from being the back-slapping politician to whom Americans were accustomed.

In addition to all this, there was his wealth. A Presidential campaign is one occasion when a rich man's money can be used against him. A certain amount of capital is helpful. But Jack's political opponents would point to the Kennedy millions and try to persuade voters that Jack was unable to sympathize with the working man.

Jack Kennedy had also made enemies, as well as friends, by his statements in favor of civil rights. He expressed the belief that all Americans — no matter what their color — were entitled to vote, to attend the same schools, and to be given the same job opportunities.

Finally, the organization working for Kennedy's election was a young one. Relatively inexperienced, it would be pitted against politics' "old pros."

Above: The Kennedy brothers, Ted, Jack, and Bobby, attend a banquet in Washington, D. C., in 1958. *Below:* JFK and his campaign manager plan their strategy during the '60 campaign.

Against these odds, Robert Kennedy worked tirelessly in his brother's behalf.

First of all, Jack had to receive the Democratic Party's nomination. A large part of Bobby's job consisted of talking with delegates who would attend the Democratic convention to choose the party's candidate. Months before the convention, he spent hours on the telephone each day phoning important delegates throughout the country. Sometimes he'd catch a plane to go see them. This enormous effort was directed toward getting a majority of the delegates to vote for Jack at the convention.

When John F. Kennedy did win the nomination, Bobby's job began all over again. This time the object was to get his brother elected. They had to wage a vigorous campaign against the Republican nominee, Richard Nixon.

The younger brother spent sleepless nights, mapping campaign strategy. Voters living in big industrial centers would be concerned about crime, and the candidate's stand on labor unions. The farmers would want to know his policies on agriculture. Veterans' organizations would like to hear his views on maintaining large military forces. Banking interests would want to hear his ideas about big business. These and scores of other special interest groups, taken together, make up America. With their conflicting goals, however, they often oppose each other.

Robert Kennedy's task, among others, was to see that the right speech was made in the right place at the right time. The delicate balance of successful politics is struck when the greatest number of people are pleased with a candidate's program while the least number are dissatisfied.

Foes as well as friends of Bobby Kennedy concede that he did a great job as political strategist. On January 20, 1961, his brother, John F. Kennedy, was inaugurated as the 35th President of the United States.

Joe Kennedy's slogan, "win, win, win," had become a prophecy.

John F. Kennedy is inaugurated President, January 1960.

4 NEW FRONTIERS

The "New Frontier" was the phrase adopted by President Kennedy to represent all the goals and challenges that lay before America. It soon came to be applied to the Administration itself, which included not only an unusual number of learned men from various fields, but also a great many young men. One of them was the new Attorney General.

Robert Kennedy had not wanted to be appointed Attorney General. He predicted that Jack's political enemies would accuse him of family favoritism if his brother — who had never actually practiced law — were given this important Cabinet post. But both Jack and "Old Joe" insisted that Bobby was the man for the job. The disagreement flared up into one of the few real arguments ever to divide the Kennedy clan. Finally, Jack pulled rank on Bobby. He reminded his younger brother that he was now talking to the

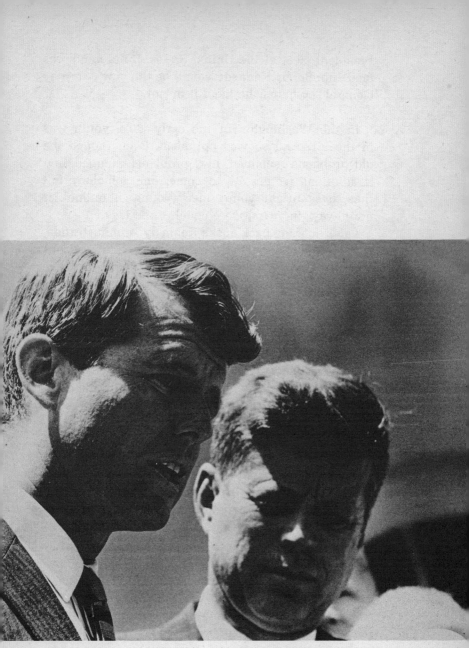

The Attorney General and the President of the United States.

President-elect of the United States. JFK's mind was made up. Bobby Kennedy would be the new Attorney General — whether he liked it or not.

In the Washington of the early '60's, youth was in the air. And so was optimism. Even though the old problems remained, new problems emerged, and if solutions were slow to come, one somehow felt that these bright young men (young in outlook if not always in years) were equal to the task.

Later, looking back at the Kennedy Administration, people remembered its youth, vigor, and gracious style of living. The arts were given a long-overdue place of honor in the capital, thanks largely to the cultivated First Lady. Even critics of the Kennedy Administration admitted that it had style.

The exuberance of the New Frontier was very much in evidence in the Justice Department. There, employees found themselves with a boss who often worked in shirtsleeves and with his feet on the desk, who sometimes — in moments of stress — tossed a football back and forth with his visitors, and who might drop by a worker's desk and introduce himself with a casual "Hi, I'm Bob Kennedy." They also got used to seeing children in the halls. Bobby's ever-growing family — which now numbered seven off-spring — frequently popped in and out of his office to see how Daddy was getting along.

Any employee who thought this cheerful informality meant that the job would be easy, soon learned better. While the Kennedys believed in playing hard, they also believed in working hard. Bobby was no exception. He worked long hours, and he demanded the same of his associates.

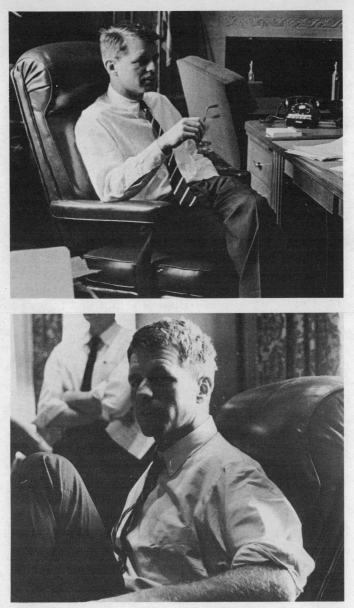

Above: the new Attorney General in his office. *Below:* May, 1961, he announces that he has sent federal marshals to Montgomery, Alabama, to quell racial violence in that city.

Robert Kennedy had taken office amid a great deal of criticism (as he'd expected) about his lack of experience. He soon began getting plenty of experience and showing that he could handle it.

The major issue he faced as Attorney General was that of civil rights. On several occasions he had to use his authority to insure Negroes' right to vote, to attend school, and to use public accommodations.

Bob Kennedy had been slow to take up the Negroes' cause as his own. But when he did, he pursued it with typical Kennedy determination.

One of the most dramatic incidents of his career as Attorney General was the James Meredith case. In September 1962, he had to send U.S. marshals and, finally, troops to Oxford, Mississippi, to enforce a Federal court order admitting James Meredith, a Negro, to the University of Mississippi. The riot that followed the registration of Meredith, the first Negro ever to attend "Ole Miss," left two dead and hundreds injured. Robert Kennedy had demonstrated that he'd meant what he said in a speech at the University of Georgia the previous year: "We will not stand by or be aloof. We will move. I happen to believe that the 1954 [school desegregation] decision was right. But my belief does not matter. It is the law. Some of you may believe the decision was wrong. That does not matter. It is the law."

At this time, many Americans felt there was a need for stronger civil rights legislation and enforcement. But this goal was hard to reach. The Administration had to cope with a Congress in which some older Southern Senators and Representatives blocked the passage of new legislation. Eventually, seven months after President Kennedy was killed, the civil rights

Washington, September, 1962: The Attorney General addresses
students employed by the federal government during vacation.

Bobby and Ethel prepare to leave on their goodwill tour.

bill he and his brother had prepared became law in President Lyndon Johnson's Administration.

In addition to serving his brother as Attorney General, Robert Kennedy served him as confidant and unofficial "Assistant President." The Presidency is a terribly lonely post. In his younger brother, John Kennedy had a friend he could trust completely, a person with whom he could share the burdens of the office.

As his brother's representative, Bobby Kennedy traveled to many countries, carrying the message of the New Frontier and, often, making new friends for the United States.

In 1962, the President sent Bobby and Ethel on a worldwide goodwill tour. A highlight of the trip was their audience with the late, beloved Pope John XXIII, who greeted them warmly.

But the welcome was not always so warm. In Japan and Indonesia, Bobby was heckled by leftist students. He held his ground and put in a firm plea for mutual respect: "I'm not asking you to agree with me," he told the Indonesians, "but I do ask that there be some understanding of us as we attempt to understand your position."

In Berlin, Bobby got a close-up look at the stark ugliness of the Wall, which the Communists had built to divide the Eastern and Western sectors of the city. The Communists were extremely sensitive to the fact that they'd had to put up the wall, not to keep outsiders out, but to prevent thousands of East Germans from seeking freedom in the West. At a City Hall rally, Robert Kennedy assured West Berliners of continued American support.

Escorted by an Indonesian nobleman, Bobby and Ethel visit
the grounds of a Hindu temple, during their 1962 goodwill tour.

Above: The couple chat with Pope John XXIII. *Below:* Kennedy at Berlin Wall with Mayor Willy Brandt (second from left).

A more serious confrontation with the Communist world was to come later that year. In October 1962, a United States U-2 reconnaissance plane flying over Cuba took a series of startling photographs. These pictures showed a Soviet missile base under construction. It was later learned that other such bases were being built elsewhere in Cuba.

These bases, if completed, would put the U.S. under the threat of close-range nuclear attack. Yet how could the Soviets be forced to stop their construction? A showdown between the big powers might precipitate a world war.

In an attempt to find a solution, President Kennedy summoned a number of his advisers. They included Defense Secretary Robert McNamara, Secretary of State Dean Rusk, CIA director John McCone, Vice President Lyndon Johnson, various military men — and Bobby Kennedy.

Not quite 37 years old, Bobby was by far the youngest Presidential adviser present. But the age and experience of older men didn't awe him, and he persistently questioned some of their advice.

A number of advisers, for instance, wanted to bomb the bases by surprise. Bobby strongly objected. "That would be like Pearl Harbor in reverse," he said. It was the Japanese sneak attack on the U.S. Naval base at Pearl Harbor, Hawaii, which had plunged this nation into World War II.

Others wanted to impose a naval blockade around Cuba. This would prevent additional Soviet missiles from being shipped there. But what about the 42 missiles already in place? They were being rapidly put into operation so that they could be fired.

After a week of these secret conferences, Bobby

Kennedy had emerged as a capable and persuasive "moderator."

On the evening of October 22, President Kennedy went on the air to tell the nation of the presence of the Soviet missiles in Cuba. He said that the U.S. would impose a blockade on further missile shipments.

The announcement put the whole world into a state of alarm. What if the Soviets failed to respect the blockade? Suddenly the nightmare of nuclear war seemed on the verge of becoming a reality.

Rumors flew. One report had it that the United States was preparing to invade Cuba. What would be the Soviet response?

After the President's announcement, many Soviet ships, bound for Cuba, turned back. But what about the missiles still being assembled in Cuba?

Finally, Soviet Premier Nikita Khrushchev sent two messages regarding this dangerous confrontation. The first was a secret message to the President. It hinted that the Soviets might be willing to remove the missiles in return for a promise from the United States not to invade Cuba. The second was broadcast over Radio Moscow. It was much tougher. It demanded that the United States remove *its* missiles from Turkey, located on the southern border of the U.S.S.R.

Bobby Kennedy then made a bold suggestion: Pretend that nobody had received the second message. Meanwhile, act as though this nation was accepting the first proposal — with one difference. The removal of the missiles should be carried out under the supervision of the United Nations.

While the world awaited Khrushchev's answer, the Soviet Ambassador in Washington added to the gloom. The Ambassador, Anatoly Dobrynin, predicted that the U.S. terms would be rejected.

But he was wrong. At 9 o'clock on Sunday morning, October 28, Khrushchev accepted the U.S. offer.

Thanks in part to Robert Kennedy's advice, the Cuban missile crisis was over. He had proved himself to be not only a capable politician but a shrewd negotiator as well.

Between the crises, after the long working hours, Bobby Kennedy shared precious moments of relaxation with friends and family. Sometimes the occasion was a rambunctious game of football with the whole clan — or one of the much publicized 50-mile hikes. Another time it might be a trip to a nearby amusement park with his children.

At Hyannis Port, or at Hickory Hill, the Robert Kennedys' home in Virginia, there were always children. And there was the sound of laughter.

Until one day in November 1963.

For John F. Kennedy, Friday, November 22, 1963, began as a cheerful day in Fort Worth, Texas. The President was in that state on a political mission — to help resolve differences within the Democratic Party.

There had been indications that the President's reception might not be altogether friendly. The civil rights issue was still a hot one, and some Texans were very critical of Kennedy. Adlai Stevenson, U.S. Ambassador to the United Nations, had recently been spat upon in Dallas; and, at this very moment, placards were being circulated bearing the President's picture and the words: "Wanted for Treason."

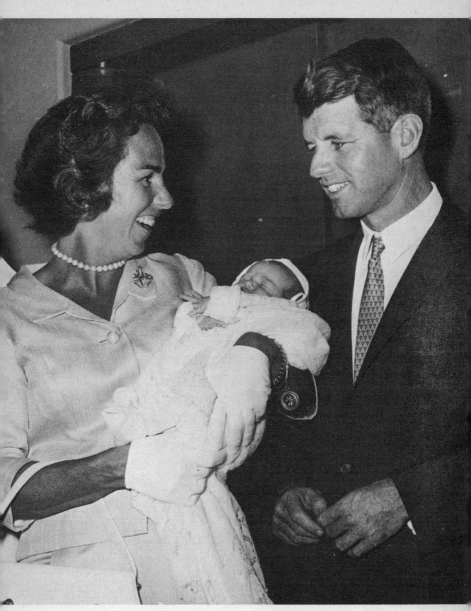

Another young Kennedy, Christopher George, with his parents.

David and Joseph Kennedy enjoy a ride on "The Whip" with their father at Glen Echo, a Maryland amusement park.

Mary Kerry Kennedy gets a better view of a ceremony on the White House lawn honoring U.S. astronaut Gordon Cooper.

Yet, so far things had gone very well. The previous day, the President and his First Lady had received warm receptions in San Antonio, Houston, and, finally, Fort Worth.

President Kennedy began this Friday by addressing a Chamber of Commerce breakfast. His wife, Jacqueline, arrived a little late. The President was in a jesting mood. As the crowd whispered and turned to see Mrs. Kennedy enter in a beautiful pink suit, the President joked, "Nobody wonders what Lyndon and I wear."

Perhaps the crowd laughed a little longer than most crowds would have at a similar remark. For "Lyndon," of course, was Texas' own Lyndon Johnson, the Vice President, who was accompanying the President.

For Mrs. Kennedy, the crowd felt warm sympathy. This was her first major public appearance since the death of the Kennedys' infant son Patrick in August. She was just recovering from the strain and sorrow of that experience.

After the Fort Worth speech, the President and his party flew to Dallas. The big Presidential jet plane set down at Love Field at 11:37 A.M.

Less than two hours later — at 1:33 P.M. — the President was pronounced dead. He had been cut down by an assassin, later identified as Lee Harvey Oswald.

Investigators said Oswald had lain in wait for the President's motorcade as it passed the Texas School Book Depository. From a sixth-floor window of this old building, Oswald had fired a rifle at President Kennedy, wounding him fatally in the head.

November 22, 1963. Robert Kennedy is comforted by his sons.

The death of the President plunged the entire free world into, first, anguished shock, and then deep mourning. But if the nation and world felt the loss, the Kennedy family felt it many times over. For they had lost — more than a vigorous and inspiring leader — a father, husband, son, and brother.

Yet it was the Kennedy family who set an example for all to follow by their brave bearing and solemn dignity during those days of sorrow.

Robert Kennedy had been at home in Virginia when it happened. Amid the confusion of that terrible day, he managed to slip away for a while to be alone with his own thoughts. At dusk, he met Jackie at the airport when she arrived with her husband's body. In the days following, he stood beside her. After the funeral service, it was Bobby who was beside Jackie when she encouraged her three-year-old son, "John-John," to give a tiny salute as his father's coffin passed. Finally, it was Bobby who assisted her as she turned from the grave at the National Cemetery with the folded flag which had draped Jack's bier.

To many people, the death of John F. Kennedy meant the end of an era. True, it had been a short one: the President had held office less than three years. But it was a time different from other times — more exciting, more full of promise.

For Bobby Kennedy, during those first empty months, it seemed as though the promise, too, had died.

The casket containing the body of the late President leaves St. Matthew's Cathedral. Beside Mrs. Kennedy are Ted, actor Peter Lawford (Pat Kennedy's former husband), and Bobby.

5 RECOVERY

For nine months after his brother's death, Robert Kennedy served as Attorney General for the new President, Lyndon B. Johnson. During much of that time, he seemed at loose ends. He had not only lost a brother, he had also lost much of his own purpose in life.

President Johnson had his own set of close personal advisers. Bobby was no longer "Assistant President." The role of Attorney General didn't seem challenging enough.

On an impulse, he reportedly once volunteered to serve as Ambassador to South Viet Nam. President Johnson is said to have refused him the post. He reasoned that the job was too dangerous. He didn't want to be responsible — even indirectly — for the death of another Kennedy.

Bobby thought about other possibilities. He con-

The New York Senate race: Bobby campaigns in Rochester, where sympathy runs high for the incumbent, Kenneth Keating.

Robert Kennedy walks toward the United States Capitol.

sidered teaching. He toyed with the idea of running for the governorship of Massachusetts.

All this while, he kept remembering his fallen brother. It seemed to him that Jack's administration had represented a time of hope, a step toward peace and brotherhood that was gradually being forgotten. "People are still looking for that idealism," he once remarked. "If I could figure out some course for me that would keep all that alive and utilize it for the country, that's what I'd do."

The idea then occurred to him to seek the Vice Presidency in the 1964 election. From there, he could later aim for the White House. He could finish what he regarded as his brother's unfinished work, his not fully realized dream.

But President Johnson didn't like the idea of seeming to be beholden to the Kennedy name. Through no fault of his, he had "inherited" the Presidency from a Kennedy. But he decided he didn't need a Kennedy as a running mate to win the next Presidential election on his own. He sidetracked Bobby's plan by announcing that no member of his Cabinet would be his Vice President.

The President's announcement seemed to spur Bobby to action. Within weeks he had resigned his Cabinet post, changed his residence to New York, and made it known that he was going back into politics. He would run for the Senate. Never before had he been a candidate for public office. But he knew how to win, and this time he would win for himself.

Bobby's decision to seek elective office in a state he had lived in only briefly brought new charges against him. He was now accused of being not only "ruthless," but a "carpetbagger" as well — one who moved from place to place to take advantage of the political situation.

But his Republican opponent — Kenneth Keating — didn't have a chance. Bobby had youth, plenty of money, an earnest way of speaking — and the magic aura of Jack Kennedy. People fought for a chance to reach out and touch him. "It's the ghost of JFK," exclaimed one sad Republican.

Bobby won the Senate seat by a whopping margin, 719,693 votes.

In his first two years as Senator, Robert Kennedy inspired a number of projects in New York State of which even a veteran legislator would be proud. These included assistance to underprivileged and emotionally disturbed school children, the establishment of a corporation to bring industry to Brooklyn slums, and the setting up of regional development councils for upstate counties.

But while the job offered him a new sense of direction, being a Senator wasn't precisely Bobby's cup of tea. For one who'd been as near the center of governmental power as he had, the chores of a legislator sometimes seemed dull. To break the monotony, Bobby began to take frequent trips, speaking out on national and international issues. It soon was rumored that he was thinking of seeking the Presidency in 1968.

The year 1968 provided many political surprises. Not the least among them was the strong showing in the New Hampshire Presidential primary made by Senator Eugene McCarthy. This genial and seasoned senator from Minnesota had announced his candidacy for the Democratic nomination to fill what he

David Kennedy campaigns for his father, who has just received the Democratic nomination for the U.S. Senate. Standing behind Kennedy is New York City Mayor Robert Wagner.

President Johnson and Bobby Kennedy campaign in Brooklyn.

Senator Kennedy testifies at a committee hearing on housing.

The Senator enjoys the skiing at Tupper Lake, New York.

considered to be a vacuum in American politics. McCarthy was a "peace" candidate, one who emphasized the need to find a negotiated settlement to the war in Viet Nam.

This had been one of Bobby's favorite themes. But the necessity to stay "alive" in politics had dictated that he soft-pedal this belief somewhat — as long as he remained a "regular" Democrat supporting President Johnson.

Bobby's keen sense of politics, which had once helped his brother become President, told him that it was too early to make his move. President Johnson was no newcomer to politics himself. A former Majority Leader of the Senate — and now the Chief Executive for more than four years — he had many powerful political friends.

Political experts seemed to agree with this thinking. President Johnson was too strong for any Democrat to "unhorse." Better for Bobby to wait until the 1972 elections. Then Johnson would be barred by the Constitution from serving another term. With the "magic" of the Kennedy name — and those additional years of experience behind him — Bobby should be a "shoo-in" for the nomination. *If* he could maintain these political advantages.

But time waits for no man — especially if he's in politics. Everything changed with McCarthy's triumph in New Hampshire. It became evident that many Democrats were in a mood for immediate change.

How could Bobby continue to sit back and watch McCarthy wage successful campaigns on the very issues about which he, Bobby, felt so strongly? Considering Bobby's temperament, the answer was

Democratic Fund-raising Dinner, 1967. *Above:* the Kennedys with actor Cary Grant (center) and comedian Alan King. *Below:* with Sen. Eugene McCarthy, Presidential candidate.

March 18, 1968. In the Senate Caucus Room, where John Kennedy made a similar statement years earlier, Bobby announces that he will seek the Democratic nomination for President.

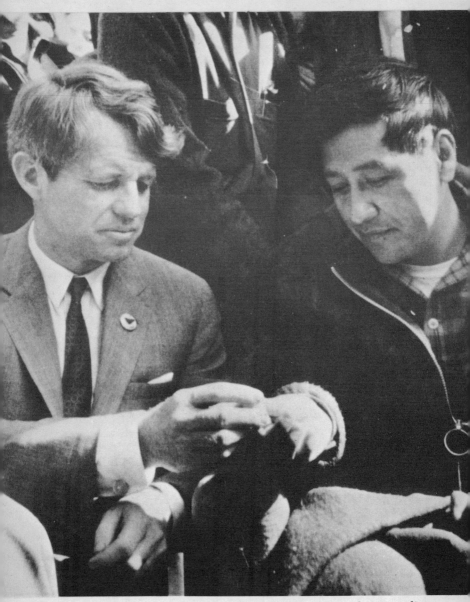

Kennedy breaks bread with union leader Cesar Chavez, ending Chavez's 23-day fast in strike against Calif. grape-growers.

obvious: he couldn't. But it would be an uphill fight to get the nomination. He wasn't nearly as sure that he could win as he had been while fighting for his brother's election. But it was now or never.

On March 18, 1968, he announced that he was a candidate for the Democratic nomination for President. Those who attended his news conference were aware that it was being held in the same Senate Caucus Room in which his late brother had made a similar announcement some eight years earlier.

With President Johnson's announcement, two weeks later, that he would not run for re-election, Bobby's prospects improved considerably.

For the rest of Robert's last campaign, he would be compared to his brother. Their speaking voices and gestures were similar. Bobby looked quite a bit like JFK. He, too, was a vote-catcher. And as Jack had before him, he pursued his Presidential dream by "going to the people" in the state primary elections — trying to prove to professional politicians his voter-appeal in primary elections, some of which were no more than popularity contests.

Following the announcement of his candidacy, Bobby entered every state primary election he lived to see. He won in the Indiana, and Washington, D.C., contests and scored smashing successes in Nebraska and South Dakota. Then he campaigned in Oregon before, finally, winning in California.

This was the point he had reached on June 5, 1968.

The Kennedys with Mr. and Mrs. John Glenn in Oregon, 1968.

A wave of the hand and the familiar boyish smile, 1968.

6 REQUIEM

"If anyone wants to kill me," Robert Kennedy once said, "it won't be difficult."

It wasn't difficult for a young man who entered the Ambassador Hotel on the night of June 5 allegedly with a revolver. Sirhan Sirhan, 24, was a Jordanian nationalist who had lived in the U.S. with his mother and brothers since 1957. An outspoken foe of Israel, he had apparently been angered by Kennedy's campaign statements supporting the United States' commitment to Israel's security.

Witnesses say Sirhan waited in the kitchen of the hotel, and asked several people if the Senator would pass that way. When Kennedy and his party entered the kitchen, the assassin reportedly slipped behind a counter, four feet away from his victim, and fired. In the chaos that followed, five other people were injured before Sirhan was overpowered and his gun removed.

June 6, 1968: Closing the RFK campaign headquarters, New York.

On June 6, while Sirhan, now under indictment for murder, sat in a Los Angeles jail, the body of Robert Kennedy was flown back to New York. Among those accompanying the body were three widows: Ethel Kennedy, Jacqueline Kennedy, and Coretta King, wife of the slain civil rights leader.

Arriving at St. Patrick's Cathedral that evening, the funeral party found a line beginning to form outside its doors. By the middle of the next day, the line was several blocks long. Thousands of people waited for hours in the sweltering heat for the privilege of walking past the casket containing the body of Robert Kennedy. From time to time, members of the Kennedy family and close friends came into the church. And all over the country, people watched these events on television, as they had watched similar events four-and-a-half years before.

They watched the following day, as the nation's leaders gathered in the cathedral for the Requiem Mass. They heard Ted Kennedy, the last and youngest of the four Kennedy sons, pay tribute to his brother in a quietly stirring eulogy.

Later, many people lined the railroad tracks between New York and Washington in order to see the funeral train pass on its way to the burial.

This final ceremony took place at Arlington Cemetery, not far from the grave of the late President John F. Kennedy.

Throughout all these events and during the days and weeks that followed, Americans asked themselves if there was not perhaps something in this country that encouraged people to try to settle their grievances

(Continued on page 93)

Mourners wait for hours to enter St. Patrick's Cathedral.

Inside the cathedral people file past Kennedy's casket.

Robert F. Kennedy, Jr., (r.) and cousin Christopher Lawford.

The widow prays beside
her husband's casket.

Ted Kennedy delivers the eulogy at his brother's funeral.

Crowds watch the funeral train pass on its way to Washington.

The burial at Arlington. The family kneel by the coffin.

through violence. The fact that Robert Kennedy's accused assassin was a foreigner did not halt the critical self-examination.

Some practical measures were taken. Secret Service protection was ordered for Presidential candidates. Gun-control legislation was proposed in Congress — and quickly bogged-down in the opposition from the well-entrenched gun lobby.

Such proposals, however, did not deal directly with the basic causes of the violence. Even the strictest firearms law would not prevent people from killing. What could be done?

Many people, despairing, said that nothing could be done. The problem seemed so huge as to be insurmountable.

Such resignation would have gotten no sympathy from Bobby Kennedy. To see a problem and not try to solve it, to abandon a struggle because of its difficulty, was to him unthinkable. Whatever goal a man would choose, he had a commitment to fight for that goal as if his life depended on it. For Bobby Kennedy, there was only one acceptable outcome: victory.

Whatever faults Robert Kennedy had, it could never be said that he did not care. Speaking at his funeral, his brother Ted had this to say:

"My brother need not be idealized or enlarged in death, beyond what he was in life, to be remembered simply as a good and decent man who saw wrong and tried to right it, saw suffering and tried to heal it, saw war and tried to stop it. . . ."